Ralph
VAUGHAN WILLIAMS

FIVE MYSTICAL SONGS

Edited by
Richard W. Sargeant, Jr.

Study Score
Partitur

SERENISSIMA MUSIC, INC.

ORCHESTRA

2 Flutes

2 Oboes

2 Clarinets (B-flat and A)

2 Bassoons

4 Horns (F)

2 Trumpets (C)*

3 Trombones

Tuba

Timpani

Harp

Violin I

Violin II

Viola

Violoncello

Double Bass

*The present score has been updated for the common keys of modern instruments
(Clarinets in A or B-flat, Horns in F, Trumpets in C).
The composer's original score featured Trumpets in F.

Duration: ca. 20 minutes

Premiere: September 14, 1911
Worcester, United Kingdom
Three Choirs Festival
Baritone solo, Festival Chorus and Orchestra / Composer

ISMN: 979-0-58042-127-2
This score is a newly engraved urtext edition prepared
from the primary sources.

Printed in the USA
First Printing: September, 2018

FIVE MYSTICAL SONGS
1. Easter

Ralph Vaughan Williams
Edited by Richard W. Sargeant, Jr.

praise, Sing his praise, With - out de - lays,
Sing his praise with-out de - lays,
Sing his praise with-out de - lays,
Sing his praise with-out de - lays,
Sing his praise with-out de - lays,
div.
unis.
pizz.
arco

14
Fl.
Ob.
Cl.
Bn.
Hn.
Tpt.
Timp.
Hp.
Bar.
Who takes thee by the hand, that thou like-wise With him may'st rise: That, as his
S.
A.
T.
B.
14
Vn.
Va.
Vc.
Cb.

death   cal - cin - ed thee to   dust,   His life   may make thee gold,   and much   more, Just.
Rise,   heart;

28
33
Fl.
Ob.
Cl.
Bn.
Hn.
Tpt.
Timp.
Hp.
Bar.
Rise, heart; thy Lord is ris - en.
S.
Rise, heart; Rise, heart; thy Lord is ris en.
A.
Rise, heart; Rise, heart; thy Lord is ris en.
T.
thy Lord is risen, Rise, heart; thy Lord is ris - en.
B.
Rise, heart; Rise, heart; thy Lord is ris - en.
Vn.
Va.
Vc.
Cb.
mf cresc.
a2
poco f
unis.
arco
42400

36
Fl. 1 2
Ob. 1 2
Cl. 1 2
Bn. 1 2
Hn. 1 2
Hn. 3 4
Tpt. 1 2
Timp.
Hp.
Bar.
S.
A.
T.
B.
Vn. 1
Vn. 2
Va.
Vc.
Cb.
p
p
p
p
p dolce
pp
p dolce
pp
pp
p
pp
div.
div.
div.
div.
p dolce
p dolce
p dolce
p dolce
p dolce
pizz.
p dolce
p dim. molto sost.
p dim. molto sost.
p dim. molto sost.
p dim. molto sost.
p dim. molto sost.
div.
arco
p dim. molto sost.
ppp
ppp
ppp
ppp
ppp
ppp

44 poco animato
1.
A - wake, my lute, and strug-gle for thy part With all thy
44 poco animato
unis.
pizz.
pizz.
arco

art.
The cross taught all wood to re - sound his name

poco rit.
a tempo
Fl.
Ob.
Cl.
Bn.
con sord.
senza sord.
Hn.
con sord.
senza sord.
Tpt.
Timp.
Hp.
Bar.
Who bore the same. His stretch-ed sin - ews taught all strings, what key Is best to
S.
A.
T.
B.
poco rit.
a tempo
Vn.
Va.
Vc.
div.
pizz.
pizz.
Cb.

poco allarg.
60 Tempo alla prima
58
Fl. 1 2
Ob. 1 2
Cl. 1 2
Bn. 1 2
Hn. 1 2
Hn. 3 4
Tpt. 1 2
Timp.
Hp.
Bar.
cel - e-brate this most high day.
S.
Con - sort both heart and
A.
Con - sort both heart and
T.
Con - sort both heart and
B.
Con - sort both heart and
poco allarg.
60 Tempo alla prima
58
Vn. 1
Vn. 2
Va.
Vc.
Cb.
pp cresc.
mf cresc.
p cresc.
f gliss.
arco

62
Fl.
Ob.
Cl.
Bn.
Hn.
Tpt.
Timp.
Hp.
Bar.
Con - sort both heart and lute, Con-sort both heart and lute, and twist a song Pleas - ant and long:
S.
lute, Con - sort both heart and lute.
A.
lute, Con-sort both heart and lute.
T.
lute, Con-sort both heart and lute.
B.
lute, Con - sort both heart and lute.
62
Vn.
div. unis.
div. unis.
Va.
unis.
Vc.
arco pizz.
Cb.
ff p pp

Largamente
Or since all mu - sic is but three parts vied, And mul - ti - plied; O let thy
O let thy
O let thy
O let thy
O let thy
Largamente
arco
pizz.

79
Fl.
Ob.
Cl.
Bn.
Hn.
Tpt.
Timp.
Hp.
Bar.
S.
A.
T.
B.
Vn.
Va.
Vc.
Cb.
pp dolce
pp
pp
pp
pp
p
dim.
più p
dim.
ppp
più p
dim.
ppp
più p
dim.
ppp
più p
dim.
ppp
pp dolce
div.
pp dolce
div.
unis.
pp dolce
arco
pizz.
bless-ed Spir - it bear a part, And make up our de-fects with his sweet
bless-ed Spir - it bear a part, with his sweet
bless-ed Spir - it bear a part, with his sweet
bless-ed Spir - it bear a part, with his sweet
bless-ed Spir - it bear a part, with his sweet
77
77
42400
15

poco rall.
82
Fl. 1 2
Ob. 1 2
Cl. 1 2
Bn. 1 2
Hn. 1 2
3 4
Tpt. 1 2
Timp.
Hp.
Bar.
S.
A.
T.
B.
poco rall.
82
Vn. 1
Vn. 2
Va.
Vc.
Cb.
ppp dim
ppp
pppp
1.
pp
con sord.
pp molto legato
ppp
pppp
p
art.
art.
art.
art.
art.
3
div.
pp dim.
ppp dim.
pppp
pp dim.
ppp dim.
pppp
pp dim. molto sost.
ppp dim.
pppp
pp dim. molto sost.
ppp dim.
pppp
pp dim. molto sost.
ppp dim.
pppp
pp dim. molto sost.
ppp dim.
pppp
div.
pp dim. molto sost.
ppp dim.
pppp
arco
pp dim. molto sost.
ppp dim.
pppp

2. I Got Me Flowers

But thou wast up by break of day, And brought'st thy sweets a - long with thee.

18
Fl. 1 2
Ob. 1 2
Cl. 1 2
Bn. 1 2
Hn. 1 2
3 4
Tpt. 1 2
Trb. 1 2
3
Tuba
Timp.
Hp.
mp colla voce
Bar.
The Sun a - ris - ing in the East, Though he give light, and the East per - fume; If they should
S.
A.
T.
B.
18
Vn. 1
pp 3 f
pp 3 f
unis. pizz.
p
unis. pizz.
p
Vn. 2
pp 3 f
unis. pizz.
p
pp 3 f
pizz.
p
Va.
div.
arco
p colla voce
arco
p colla voce
Vc.
arco
p colla voce
div.
arco
p colla voce
Cb.
p

33 poco più lento
27
Fl. 1 2
Ob. 1 2
Cl. 1 2
Bn. 1 2
1.
p
p
p
Hn. 1 2
3 4
Tpt. 1 2
Trb. 1 2
Tuba 3
Timp.
Hp.
Bar.
of - fer to con - test. With thy a - ris - ing, they pre - sume.
Can there be an - y day but this,
pp
S.
(humming tone)*
pp
A.
(humming tone)*
pp
T.
(humming tone)*
pp
B.
(humming tone)*
33 poco più lento
27
Vn. 1
arco 3 desks
pp
2
arco 3 desks
pp
Va.
2 desks
pp
pp
Vc.
2 desks
pp
Cb.
arco 2 desks
p
pp

39 Largamente
35
Fl. 1 2
Ob. 1 2
Cl. 1 2
to A cl.
Bn. 1 2
Hn. 1 2
Hn. 3 4
Tpt. 1 2
mf sost.
Trb. 1 2
mf sost.
Tuba 3
mf sost.
Timp.
mf
Hp.
Bar.
Though ma - ny suns to shine en - deav - our? We count three hun - dred, but we miss: There is but one, and that one ev - er.
S.
There is but one, and that one ev - er.
A.
There is but one, and that one ev - er.
T.
There is but one, and that one ev - er.
B.
There is but one, and that one ev - er.
39 Largamente
35
tutti pizz. arco
Vn. 1
tutti pizz. arco
Vn. 2
tutti pizz. arco
Va.
tutti pizz. arco
Vc.
tutti pizz. arco
Cb.

3. Love Bade Me Welcome

18 Largamente
Fl. 1 2
Ob. 1 2
Cl. 1 2
1.
p dolce
Bn. 1 2
pp
pp
Hn. 1 2
ppp
pp
largamente
Bar.
wel-come; yet my soul drew back, Guil-ty of dust and sin. But quick-eyed Love, ob-serv-ing me grow slack From my first en-trance in, Drew
S.
A.
T.
B.
18 Largamente
Vn. 1
Vn. 2
Va.
pp
Vc.
pizz.
Cb.
pp

a tempo
19
Fl. 1 2
pp
p dolce
1.
Ob. 1 2
p dolce 3
1.
Cl. 1 2
3
p dolce
p dolce
Bn. 1 2
pp
Hn. 1 2
pp
pp
Bar.
near-er to me, sweet - ly ques-tion-ing, If I lack'd an-y thing. "A guest," I an-swer'd, "worth-y to be here:"
S.
A.
T.
B.
a tempo
19
ten.
Vn. 1
pp
p dolce
ten.
2
pp
p dolce
ten.
Va.
p dolce
pizz. arco
ten.
Vc.
pp
p dolce
arco
Cb.
pp

33
poco animato
Fl. 1 2
Ob. 1 2
Cl. 1 2
Bn. 1 2
Hn. 1 2
Bar.
S.
A.
T.
B.
Vn. 1
Vn. 2
Va.
Vc.
Cb.
p
mf
pp
p
pp
ppp
pp
1.
pp
mf
p
pp
ppp
1.
pp
con sord.
senza sord.
mf
p
pp
poco f
pp
Love said, "You shall be he." "I the un-kind, un-grate-ful? Ah, my dear, I can-not look on thee."
33
poco animato
div.
unis.
pp
mf
p
pp
pp dolce
div.
unis.
pp
mf
p
pp dolce
pizz.
arco
f
p
pp dolce
unis.
pizz.
div.
unis.
arco
pp
f
pp dolce
pizz.
arco
f
pp
pp dolce

Love took my hand, and smil - ing did re - ply, "Who made the eyes but I?" "Truth, Lord, but I have marr'd them: let my shame

colla voce
largamente
52 Tempo I
poco allarg.
a tempo
Fl. 1 2
p dolce
ppp
Ob. 1 2
1.
p dolce
pp
Cl. 1 2
p colla voce
ppp
pp
Bn. 1 2
p colla voce
pp
con sord. (not brassy)
Hn. 1 2
p colla voce
p dolce
con sord. (not brassy)
pp
Bar.
p largamente
p dolce
Go where it doth de - serve.
"And know you not," says Love, "who bore the blame?"
S.
A.
T.
B.
colla voce
largamente
52 Tempo I
poco allarg.
a tempo
Vn. 1
p colla voce
pp
pp dolce
Vn. 2
p colla voce
pp dolce
div.
unis.
Va.
p colla voce
pp dolce
Vc.
p colla voce
pp dolce
1 desk
p colla voce
pp dolce
pp
Cb.
p colla voce
tutti
(pizz.)
arco
pp
p colla voce
pp dolce
pp
49

colla voce   a tempo (largamente)   rit.   64   a tempo
58
Fl. 1 2
poco f
Ob. 1 2
poco f
Cl. 1 2
poco f
pp
ppp
1.
pppp
Bn. 1 2
poco f
pp
ppp
Hn. 1 2
f
pp
ppp
Bar.
largamente
f
"My dear,   then   I   will   serve."
(cue to seated chorus)
pppp (senza espress.)
S.
Ah
pppp (senza espress.)
A.
Ah
pppp (senza espress.)
T.
Ah
pppp (senza espress.)
B.
Ah
colla voce   a tempo (largamente)   rit.   64   a tempo
58
div.
Vn. 1
f
p colla voce   pp
ppp
2
f
p colla voce   pp
ppp
solo
senza sord.
Va.
f
p colla voce   pp
pppp senza espress.
tutti
f
p colla voce   pp
ppp
Vc.
f
p colla voce   pp
ppp   ppp
f
p colla voce   pp
ppp   ppp
unis.
pizz.
Cb.
f
p colla voce   pp
ppp

colla voce   a tempo
Fl. 1 2
Ob. 1 2
Cl. 1 2
Bn. 1 2
Hn. 1 2
pppp
pppp
ppp
Bar.
pp dolce
pp
"You must sit down," says Love, "and taste my meat:"
So I did sit
S.
pppp
Ah
A.
pppp
Ah
T.
pppp
Ah
B.
pppp
Ah
colla voce   a tempo
Vn. 1
Vn. 2
sempre ppp
Va.
pppp
sempre ppp
Vc.
sempre ppp
arco
sempre ppp
pizz.
Cb.
ppp

79
77
Fl. 1 2
Ob. 1 2
Cl. 1 2
Bn. 1 2
Hn. 1 2
Bar.
S.
A.
T.
B.
Vn. 1 2
Va.
Vc.
Cb.
pppp
pppp
1.
ppp
1.
ppp
and eat.
pppp
Ah
Ah
pppp
Ah
Ah
pppp
Ah
Ah
pppp
Ah
Ah
79
77
ppp
sempre ppp
pppp
sempre ppp
3
3
sempre ppp
sempre ppp

poco rall.
86
Fl. 1 2
Ob. 1 2
Cl. 1 2
to B♭ cl.
ppp
Bn. 1 2
1.
pppp
Hn. 1 2
2. senza sord.
1. (con sord.)
senza sord.
ppp
ppp
Bar.
S.
A.
T.
B.
poco rall.
86
Vn. 1
div.
cantabile
ppp
cantabile
ppp
pppp
nothing
senza sord.
pppp
nothing
senza sord.
Vn. 2
senza sord.
Va.
pp cantible
div.
pp cantible
ppp
senza sord.
nothing
Vc.
ppp
ppp
nothing
senza sord.
ppp
ppp
nothing
senza sord.
Cb.
senza sord.

4. The Call

Lento moderato
Flute 1 2
Oboe 1 2
Clarinet in B♭
Bassoon 1 2
Horn (F) 1 2
Harp
Solo Baritone
Come, my Way, my Truth, my Life: Such a Way, as gives us breath: Such a
Lento moderato
Violin 1
div.
Violin 2
div.
solo
Viola
div.
solo
Violoncello
div.
solo
Contrabass
solo
p

13
Fl. 1 2
Ob. 1 2
Cl. 1 2
Bn. 1 2
Hn. 1 2
Hp.
Bar.
Vn. 1
Vn. 2
Va.
Vc.
Cb.
p
p
p
p
p
tutti
pp
tutti
pp
pp
pp
tutti
pp
tutti
pp
tutti
pp
tutti
pp
pizz.
pp
1.
Truth, as ends all strife: Such a Life, as kill - - - eth death.
Come, my Light, my Feast, my

Strength: Such a Light, as shows a feast: Such a Feast, as mends in length: Such a Strength, as makes his

poco animato
23
21
Fl. 1 2
Ob. 1 2
Cl. 1 2
Bn. 1 2
Hn. 1 2
Hp.
Bar.
mf
p
f
mf
f
mf
mf
p
f
mf
f
guest.
Come, my Joy, my Love, my Heart: Such a Joy, as none can move:
poco animato
23
21
Vn. 1
Vn. 2
Va.
Vc.
Cb.
con sord.
con sord.
con sord.
con sord.
con sord.
con sord.
f
f
f
f
pizz.
f
mf
sordini poco a poco
con sord.
arco
p
* div. à 3
pizz.
f
mf
sordini poco a poco
con sord.
arco
p
pizz.
mf
con sord.
sordini poco a poco
p
* Violoncellos divide:
1st part, desks 1 & 4
2nd part, desks 2 & 5
3rd part, desks 3 & 6
42400

rall.   Tempo I   tranquillo
Fl. 1 2
Ob. 1 2
Cl. 1 2
Bn. 1 2
Hn. 1 2
Hp.
pp
p
pp
Bar.
Such a Love, as none can part: Such a Heart, as joys
2
in love.
rall.   Tempo I   tranquillo
Vn. 1
p
ppp
pppp
nothing
p
ppp
pppp
nothing
Vn. 2
p
ppp
pppp
nothing
p
ppp
pppp
nothing
Va.
p
ppp
pppp
nothing
p
ppp
pppp
nothing
Vc.
ppp
pppp
nothing
ppp
pppp
nothing
arco
Cb.
ppp

5. Antiphon

Allegro
Flute 1 2
Oboe 1 2
Clarinet in B♭
Bassoon 1 2
Horn (F) 1 2
3 4
Trumpet (C) 1 2
Trombone 1 2
Tuba 3
Timpani
Soprano
Alto
Tenor
Bass
Allegro
Violin 1
2
Viola
Violoncello
Contrabass
a2
mf cresc.
p cresc.
pp
f

15
11
Fl. 1 2
Ob. 1 2
Cl. 1 2
Bn. 1 2
a2
f marc.
ff
mf
Hn. 1 2
3 4
ff
mf
Tpt. 1 2
p
ff
Trb. 1 2
p
ff
Tuba 3
p
ff
Timp.
p
ff
S.
A.
T.
f risoluto
Let all the world in ev - ery cor - ner sing,
B.
f risoluto
Let all the world in ev - ery cor - ner sing,
15
11
Vn. 1
f
ff
2
f
ff
mf
Va.
f
ff
Vc.
f
ff
mf
Cb.
f
ff
mf

Let all the world in ev - ery cor - ner sing, My God and King.
Let all the world in ev - ery cor - ner sing, My God and King.
Let all the world in ev - ery cor - ner sing, My God and King.
Let all the world in ev - ery cor - ner sing, My God and King.

33
The heavens are not too
mf legato
The heavens are not too
mf legato
f dim.
pp
ff
pp
ff
f
pp
f dim.
pp
p
p
p
p
f dim.
f dim.
f dim.
f dim.
f dim.
29

37
Fl.
Ob.
Cl.
Bn.
Hn.
Tpt.
Trb.
Tuba
Timp.
S.
A.
T.
B.
Vn.
Va.
Vc.
Cb.
high, His praise may thi - ther fly:
high, His praise may thi - ther fly:
The earth is
The earth is
p dolce

45
Fl.
Ob.
Cl.
Bn.
p dolce
p cresc.
Hn.
p dolce
f
f cresc.
f
f cresc.
Tpt.
Trb.
Tuba
Timp.
S.
A.
not too low, His prai - ses there may grow. Let all the
f
T.
Let all the world
f
B.
not too low, His prai - ses there may grow. Let all the
45
Vn.
cresc.
cresc.
Va.
cresc.
Vc.
cresc.
Cb.
cresc.

Let all the world in ev-ery cor - - - ner sing,
world in ev-ery cor - - - ner sing,
Let all the world in ev-ery cor - - - ner sing,
world in ev - - ery cor - - - ner sing,

67
62
Fl. 1 2
f marc. cresc. ff f
Ob. 1 2
f marc. cresc. ff f
Cl. 1 2
f marc. cresc. ff f
Bn. 1 2
a2
f marc. cresc. ff f
Hn. 1 2
ff poco f
Hn. 3 4
ff poco f
Tpt. 1 2
1.
Trb. 1 2
p cresc. ff poco f
p cresc. ff
Tuba 3
p cresc. ff
Timp.
p cresc. ff
S.
f risoluto
Let all the world in ev - ery cor - ner
A.
f risoluto
Let all the world in ev - ery cor - ner
T.
f risoluto
Let all the world in ev - ery cor - ner
B.
f risoluto
Let all the world in ev - ery cor - ner
67
62
Vn. 1
f cresc. ff f
Vn. 2
f cresc. ff f
Va.
f cresc. ff f
Vc.
f cresc. ff f
Cb.
f cresc. ff f

79
sing, My God and King.
sing, My God and King.
sing, My God and King.
sing, My God and King.
42400

The Church with psalms must shout, No door can keep them out:
The Church with psalms must shout, No door can keep them out:

poco più tranquillo
90
95 a tempo
Fl. 1 2
Ob. 1 2
Cl. 1 2
Bn. 1 2
pp
pp
pp
f
f
f
f marc.
Hn. 1 2
Hn. 3 4
Tpt. 1 2
Trb. 1 2
Tuba 3
Timp.
1.
3.
pp
pp
f marc.
f marc.
S.
A.
T.
B.
p dolce
p dolce
p dolce
p dolce
But a - bove all, the heart Must bear the long - - - est part.
But a - bove all, the heart Must bear the long - - est part.
But a - bove all, the heart Must bear the long - - - est part.
But a - bove all, the heart Must bear the long - - - est part.
f risoluto
Let all the
poco più tranquillo
90
95 a tempo
Vn. 1
Vn. 2
Va.
Vc.
Cb.
pp subito
pp subito
pp subito
pp subito
pp subito
pizz.
arco
3
3
pp
pp
pp
pp
pp
f
f
f
f
f

poco animato
98
Fl. 1 2
Ob. 1 2
Cl. 1 2
Bn. 1 2
Hn. 1 2
Hn. 3 4
Tpt. 1 2
Trb. 1 2
Tuba 3
Timp.
S.
A.
T.
B.
Vn. 1
Vn. 2
Va.
Vc.
Cb.
a2
f marc.
dim.
pp
p
a2
f marc.
dim.
pp
dim.
pp
1.
mf
pp
p
f risoluto
dim.
p
Let all the world in ev - ery cor - ner ev - ery
f risoluto
dim.
Let all the world in ev - ery cor - ner sing, Let all the world
f risoluto
dim.
p
Let all the world Let all the world in ev - ery
f
dim.
p
world in ev - ery cor - ner sing, Let all the world in ev - ery cor -
poco animato
98
f
f
f marc.
dim.
p

Largamente
112 Tempo I
106
Fl. 1 2
Ob. 1 2
Cl. 1 2
Bn. 1 2
Hn. 1 2
Hn. 3 4
Tpt. 1 2
Trb. 1 2
Tuba 3
Timp.
S.
A.
T.
B.
a2
ff
pp
pp molto cresc.
mf cresc.
f
cor - ner sing, My God and King. My God and
sing, My God and King. My God and
cor - ner sing, My God and King. My God and
ner sing, My God and King. My God and
Vn. 1
Vn. 2
Va.
Vc.
Cb.
p
Largamente 112 Tempo I

poco più lento
124 Tempo I
117
Fl. 1 2
Ob. 1 2
obbligato
Cl. 1 2
a2
obbligato
a2
Bn. 1 2
obbligato
a2
Hn. 1 2
obbligato
3 4
obbligato
Tpt. 1 2
mf cresc.
ff
Trb. 1 2
mf cresc.
ff
Tuba 3
mf cresc.
ff
ff
Timp.
mf cresc.
ff
ff
S.
ff marcato
King. Let all the world in e-ve-ry cor-ner sing, My God and King.
A.
ff marcato
King. Let all the world in e-ve-ry cor-ner sing, My God and King.
T.
ff marcato
King. Let all the world in e-ve-ry cor-ner sing, My God and King.
B.
ff marcato
King. Let all the world in e-ve-ry cor-ner sing, My God and King.
poco più lento
124 Tempo I
117
Vn. 1
fff
ff
2
fff
ff
Va.
fff
ff
Vc.
fff
ff
Cb.
fff
ff
* to be played at conductor's discretion

127
Fl. 1 2
Ob. 1 2
Cl. 1 2
Bn. 1 2
Hn. 1 2
3 4
Tpt. 1 2
Trb. 1 2
Tuba 3
Timp.
S.
A.
T.
B.
Vn. 1
Vn. 2
Va.
Vc.
Cb.
a2
a2
p cresc.
ff
p cresc.
ff
p cresc.
ff
p cresc.
ff
p cresc.
ff
ff
ff
ff
p
ff
div.
mf
ff
mp cresc.
ff
mp cresc.
ff
p cresc.
ff
p cresc.
ff
div.
p cresc.
ff
127